All Aboard!
Passenger Trains Around the World

Karl Zimmermann

Photography by the author

Boyds Mills Press

In loving memory of my mother,
my first train companion

Acknowledgments

The photographs on pages 6, 21, and 24 are by Laurel Zimmermann. My thanks to her for these, of course, but also for being with me when many other photographs in this book were made—and for so much else.

The photographs on page 12 are from the Burlington Northern Santa Fe Archives. I'm grateful for permission to use them here.

—K. Z.

Published by Boyds Mills Press, Inc.
A Highlights Company
815 Church Street
Honesdale, Pennsylvania 18431
Printed in China

CIP data is available

First edition, 2004
The text of this book is set in 13-point Minion.
Visit our Web site at www.boydsmillspress.com

10 9 8 7 6 5 4 3 2 1

Contents

The conductor — called a "guard" in Europe — welcomes passengers aboard the elegant Venice Simplon-Orient-Express.

Introduction

A "Magic Carpet Made of Steel"

MANY YEARS AGO, EDNA ST. VINCENT MILLAY published "Travel," a poem that I took to heart. "Yet there isn't a train I wouldn't take," she wrote, "No matter where it's going." All my life I've happily followed that philosophy.

I was very young when I discovered the magic of rail travel, with its ever-changing views out the window. Whether soaring mountains or city streets, railroad yards or lonely farmsteads, there was always something to see. Once aboard, I looked forward to every visit to the dining car for fresh-cooked meals served on tables laid with snowy linens, gleaming silver, and fresh flowers. The waiters there were always friendly, at least in my recollections, and were especially attentive to children.

Best of all, I liked sleeping on the train, in a private space that the railroads called a "double bedroom," with upper and lower berths. "Made down" for the night, those beds were cozy nests of crisp sheets spread with brown woolen blankets that read "The Pullman Company," the operator of the nation's sleeping cars.

Fortunately for me, passenger trains were a routine, recurring part of my life as I grew up in New Jersey. My mother came from Salt Lake City, and she and I would make yearly visits to her family there.

◀ *A freak October snowstorm blankets the* American Orient Express *in Denver.*

With five Vista-Dome cars, the California Zephyr (which entered service in 1949) rolls eastbound through Colorado's Gore Canyon.

In those days, the late 1940s and 1950s, flying was an option, but travel by train remained the more obvious choice. So each year, when summer rolled around, my father would take us to the station — usually Grand Central Terminal or Pennsylvania Station in New York City — where we would board either the New York Central's *20th Century Limited* or the Pennsylvania Railroad's *Broadway Limited* for Chicago.

How exciting the bustle in those great, soaring stations, the swirl of boarding passengers! And how important I felt as we walked along the train to find our sleeping car! This was particularly true in Grand Central, where a red carpet was unrolled every night to welcome passengers aboard the *Century*. Our porter (as sleeping-car attendants were called) would greet us at the vestibule door. He'd carry our bags to our room. He'd take my mother's hat from her, put it in a

paper sack for safekeeping, and stow it overhead. He'd ask us our plans for the morning, so he'd know when to be at our door with a wake-up call.

The bedroom was tiny, but I liked it all the better for its ingenious compactness. By day it had just a single sofa seat or two individual chairs, with a portable table added if I wanted a place to play cards. After dinner my mother would buzz for the porter, who'd come and transform the room for sleep. Sometimes I'd climb the ladder into the upper berth, where crisscrossed cloth straps provided a fence to keep me from falling out.

Other times my mother would let me have the lower berth. On those occasions I slept less, since I couldn't resist pushing up the shade and watching the night-dark countryside blur past. I liked to imagine the lives of the people in the isolated farmhouses I'd see, their porch lights yellow pools of bright humanity in the blackness.

Eventually, bathed in the soft blue of the room's night-light, I would fall asleep — only to awaken at dawn to the foreign Midwestern flatness of farm fields. This overnight transformation of the familiar landscape I'd left behind always seemed to me a small miracle.

The Trains of the West

After spending the midday in Chicago, I had another priceless night and day of rail riding ahead, usually on Union Pacific's *City of Los Angeles* or the glittering, stainless-steel *California Zephyr*, jointly operated by three different railroads — the Burlington Route, the Denver & Rio Grande Western, and the Western Pacific. These Western trains had something special that most of those east of Chicago lacked: dome cars.

These cars were crowned with glassed-in observatories for 360-degree viewing. I'd scramble for a seat in the first row, and once I had it I hated to leave. I'd watch the prairies and, further west, mountains. Even more interesting to me was the unfolding world of railroading — the small-town depots, the engine terminals, the freight yards where trains of boxcars, flatcars, reefers, tank cars, stock cars, and hoppers were broken up and reassembled to continue their cross-country journeys.

I'd stare down the track, always hoping that a headlight would appear, indicating an upcoming "meet" with a passenger or freight train headed in the opposite direction. After dark, I never tired of watching as the "block signals" that controlled train movements on the line flipped from green to red as our locomotive passed them.

This magic of the rails still captivates me. When I grew

Passengers place their orders aboard the dining car of the Venice Simplon-Orient-Express.

In Australia, the Indian Pacific's *lounge car provides a comfortable place to read or watch the passing scenery.*

In the typically tiny dining-car kitchen of the American Orient Express, *the chef holds a pan of fresh oysters.*

Aboard the Indian Pacific, *a sleeping compartment is set up for day use. At night,* ▶ *the sofa converts to a lower berth and an upper berth folds out from the wall above.*

up, I continued to ride trains, by that time on my own. My honeymoon trip — to The Homestead in Virginia, a hotel once owned by the Chesapeake & Ohio Railway — was by train. Then came vacation and sometimes business travel that traversed all the states of the Union (except Hawaii), and all six of the continents that have rails.

Riding the Rails of Six Continents

I rode narrow-gauge steam trains high into the mountains of Ecuador and Guatemala and across the vast open plains of Argentina's Patagonia. I sped through the Channel Tunnel, often called the Chunnel, aboard Eurostar and rode France's lightening-fast TGVs. I rode across the breadth of Australia on the *Indian Pacific*, named for the two oceans it links. In

South Africa, I was pampered aboard the opulent *Blue Train* and *Pride of Africa*. Humble or grand, far-flung or local, each train journey added something to my sum of rail wanderings. I saw sights and met people that I otherwise would have missed.

In 1970, singer-songwriter Steve Goodman wrote "Ridin' on the City of New Orleans," inspired by a trip he and his wife had made aboard that Chicago–New Orleans streamliner, operated by Illinois Central. "This train's got the disappearin' railroad blues," Goodman wrote, lamenting the demise of rail passenger service in America. The great trains had been dying one by one, and the following year Amtrak would take over operation of those few that remained.

Fortunately, even in America, passenger trains have proven better survivors than Goodman's song predicted, and many — including Amtrak's *City of New Orleans* — still run today, with sleepers and diners and cars much like domes. But when Goodman sang of the train as a "magic carpet made of steel," he was right on target, for passenger trains can indeed whisk us away on spectacular journeys.

A narrow-gauge train nicknamed the "Old Patagonian Express" steams across southern Argentina with the snowcapped Andes in the background.

One

From Primitive to Plush

IN THEIR VERY EARLIEST YEARS, the 1830s, American passenger trains were nothing like those that we know today. They were slow. They were uncomfortable. They were dangerous. And they operated for distances that today would seem laughably short — sometimes little more than a dozen miles.

America's first passenger trains were hauled by horses, on the Baltimore & Ohio between Baltimore and Ellicott City, Maryland, beginning in 1830. In January of the next year, the South Carolina Railroad initiated the first scheduled passenger train to be pulled by a steam locomotive.

Soon to follow were trains on the Mohawk & Hudson, which ran for seventeen miles between Albany and Schenectady, New York; the Camden & Amboy in New Jersey; and many other little railroads. In the decades ahead, they would join together to form great cross-country systems that operated passenger trains between distant cities.

When passenger trains were first developed, there was, of course, no tradition of what a railway coach should be. The closest models that early builders could find were wagons and stagecoaches, so that's what they copied. Some of the first cars lacked even roofs to protect passengers from the elements — and from hot cinders drifting back

◀ *On April Fool's Day in 1959, this local train from London, Ontario — informally called the* ■ 11
"Businessman's Special" — pulls into Toronto behind a steam locomotive for the last time. The next day
diesels would take over for good. The train is a mix of streamlined and "heavyweight" cars.

Waiters and steward stand at attention aboard this diner from the wooden-car era.

from the wood-burning steam locomotive ahead. Some had no seats, and where there were seats they might well be unpadded. Typically, the cars jolted along on four wheels without springs.

Stagecoach-inspired cars, like those first operated on the Baltimore & Ohio and Mohawk & Hudson, had all the disadvantages of the road vehicles on which they were modeled. Though "swell-sided" — bulging, rather like melons — they were cramped. In common with all the early rail coaches, they had no lighting, no heat, no toilet facilities. Their passengers lacked what would turn out to be one of rail travel's great assets: the ability to easily leave your seat and move around.

Railroading was growing up fast, however. By 1837, two hundred new lines were under construction. Coaches were evolving, too, getting bigger, more spacious, and more comfortable. Already B&O was operating 32-foot-long cars

On the Atchison, Topeka & Santa Fe Railway, conductor and brakeman stand in front of their train's wooden cars, while engineer and fireman pose aboard the American Standard-type locomotive.

Wooden coaches are still used today on some railroads that haul tourists and rail enthusiasts. This train running through Colorado's Animas Canyon belongs to the Durango & Silverton Narrow-Gauge Railroad. The first-class "parlor car" at the end of the train was built in 1880.

with forty-four padded seats flanking a center aisle. (Typically, the very first cars had been about 15 feet long and seated fifteen.) Most coaches no longer rode on four wheels but on eight, in sprung, four-wheel assemblies called "trucks." Windows had gained glass.

As passenger trains began to run over longer distances, that meant more travel after dark — and more need for illumination in the coaches. For many years, that was provided by candles, often only a few per car. By the 1860s, oil lamps were common, as was kerosene. The first truly successful railway lighting was by gas — in particular, "Pintsch gas" fixtures, developed by Julius Pintsch, a German. By the 1890s these were in nearly universal use. Next would come electricity.

Sleeping and Dining on Rails

Longer trips also led to the development of sleeping cars and dining cars — two especially attractive aspects of train travel. The great name in sleeping cars was Pullman — for George M. Pullman, who didn't invent sleepers (though he often gets credit for doing so) but popularized and then marketed them so successfully that his company effectively cornered the market.

Far from the first, his *Pioneer* of 1865 nonetheless became hugely famous for its spacious luxury. In addition, it was said to have carried President Abraham Lincoln's body from Washington to Springfield, Illinois, as part of his funeral train. Though today's historians question this bit of Pullman lore, the *Pioneer* is often credited with ushering in the elegance of the "Palace Car" era. Its plush interior, paneled in black walnut, contained two staterooms and twelve "open sections" — facing seats by day that could be "made down" at night into an upper and a lower berth, hung with curtains for privacy.

The wooden cars of this White Pass & Yukon excursion train — shown here about to cross from Alaska into British Columbia — were built in the 1880s.

Now that rail travelers could sleep comfortably, the next challenge was feeding them in comparable style. Up until then, passengers had eaten during stops made along the way so that the train's locomotive could be fueled and watered. These meal stops were rushed, and the food and service at the lunchrooms generally poor. Clearly the elite who rode the ornate Palace Cars expected more.

The first successful dining in motion was on hotel cars, such as Pullman's *President* of 1867. This car had a 3-by-6-foot kitchen, a pantry, and a wine cellar. Tables were placed at the seats in the "sections" at mealtimes, then removed. The car's porter served as waiter. This arrangement had its drawbacks, however, including food smells that lingered in what became a sleeping space.

The answer was a car solely dedicated to dining, and in 1868 Pullman once more led the way, with the *Delmonico*, named after a famous restaurant in New York City. Running in the Midwest on the Chicago & Alton, this dining car was highly satisfactory, but it didn't lead to a stampede among other railroads to introduce meal service on their own trains.

That may seem odd to those who've experienced firsthand the pleasure of dining on rails, but the explanation was simple: money. Dining cars were expensive to build, staff, and operate. They were heavy, and thus expensive to haul. If competing lines didn't have them, why need we? So the railroads held back.

In fact, in all the years that dining cars have operated, right up to the present, they've always lost money. Railroad companies came to believe that diners were a requirement of first-class service, however, and a way to make their own trains stand out. This thinking justified the losses they produced, and

— in the course of the 1880s — first Western and then Eastern railroads fell into line, and dining cars became the integral part of long-distance train travel that they remain today.

Enter the "Heavyweights"

Throughout these many decades of improvements, rail passenger cars were built of wood. At first essentially all wood,

The last two cars in this train date from the "standard" or "heavyweight" era, which began in the early years of the twentieth century. The car with the open observation platform is a "business" or "office car" once used by railroad executives.

they were later of "composite" construction, with some elements, such as framing and underbody, made of steel. Again the railroads dragged their heels, moving only grudgingly to all-steel coaches, which clearly were safer in a crash or fire. No doubt management simply resisted a change that would make existing car fleets obsolete.

The breakthrough came in 1907, when the Pennsylvania Railroad was tunneling under the Hudson River from New Jersey to reach the magnificent new station it was building in New York City. A. J. Cassatt, PRR's president, felt that steel cars were essential for safety in the tunnels. Within five years, PRR had nearly three thousand steel cars in service, and other railroads had little choice but to follow suit. Thus the "standard" or "heavyweight" era was born.

These cars were impressive, smooth-riding vehicles. Most sleepers were painted a somewhat drab "Pullman Green." With their riveted sides and six-wheel trucks (wheelsets), they were imposing and substantial, if somber, battleships of the rails, as they were sometimes called.

In the teens and "Roaring Twenties," railroad passenger service in America reached its greatest heights. The economy boomed, and more Americans than ever before had the money to travel in style. Trains served one hundred thousand communities, and 95 percent of the population had easy access to a depot. Trains like the *20th Century Limited* typically ran in multiple sections — with a given day's "train" actually being as many as four or five trains, one following right behind the other.

Then, in 1929, the stock market crashed and everything changed.

Pullman and His Company

George Mortimer Pullman was born in Brocton, New York, in 1831. After working as a cabinetmaker, then taking over his late father's business of moving buildings, he left for Chicago in 1855. By then, that city had already begun to assume its role as the railroad center of America.

In Chicago, Pullman made a successful career of moving buildings — or sometimes just raising them above the advancing waters of Lake Michigan. But his real calling — which would make his name a household word for more than a century, with "Pullman" entering everyday vocabulary as a synonym for "sleeping car" — would be rail-car building.

Actually, Pullman's genius was more as an entrepreneur than a builder. Though his *Pioneer* wasn't the first sleeping car, the Pullman Palace Car Company he founded in 1867 would come to dominate and later monopolize the industry.

George Pullman named the Hotel Florence in his company town after his only daughter and favorite child. Legend has it that he also allowed her to choose the names for his sleeping cars.

Clover Colony, a classic heavyweight Pullman, contained eight "open sections" (uppers and lowers) and five "double bedrooms."

In time all competitors — there were once thirty-nine of them, including T. T. Woodruff & Company (the true pioneer, which later became the Central Transportation Company), Wagner Palace Car Company, the Mann Boudoir Car Company, and others — were squeezed out or taken over.

Pullman built his sleeping cars. He owned them. And he operated them, employing directly the conductors and porters who staffed them. From passengers he collected fares in addition to what they paid the railroads for basic transportation.

In 1881 he opened his company town of Pullman, Illinois, just south of Chicago. This community — complete with church, library, hotel, stables, shops, and housing from humble to grand — was in some ways a utopian village.

However, Pullman insisted that it return a profit, just like his other enterprises. In 1893, when the economy weakened and car orders plummeted, he laid off workers and slashed wages — without dropping rents. This led to the bloody Pullman Strike of 1894, which spread to railroads across the country.

When he died in 1897, George Pullman was more hated than admired. But his company had many great years ahead. At its peak in the latter 1920s, The Pullman Company (as it was called by then) operated ninety-eight hundred cars and hosted on average roughly fifty-five thousand passengers each night. This made Pullman the country's greatest innkeeper by far.

Two

Streamliners Take the Country by Storm

IN THE WAKE OF THE STOCK MARKET CRASH came the Great Depression. Across the country, industrial production plummeted. By 1932, roughly a quarter of America's workers were unemployed. Railroads suffered mightily in all this. Not only were there fewer goods to haul than in the boom years just ended, there also were many fewer individuals with the money to travel — or the need to, for that matter.

Passenger trains were in decline — not only because of the ailing economy but also because they appeared hopelessly old-fashioned compared with the competition, airplanes and automobiles, which were gaining rapidly in popularity. Black steam engines and drab green coaches seemed stodgy and suggested to the public the discredited past, not a bright, hopeful future. They seemed a part of the problem, not a solution.

But railroading had an answer, and that answer was streamliners — trains that would be colorful, sleek, and shiny instead of dull and boxy.

In fact, streamlining in general caught the fancy of 1930s Americans, who yearned desperately for a future brighter than the somber present. A new profession sprang up, men called "industrial

◀ *Though operating into the twenty-first century, the* American Orient Express *is a classic streamliner with cars dating to the 1940s and 1950s. Here it curves across the Utah desert in late afternoon.*

Among the relatively few streamliners powered by steam locomotives was Norfolk & Western's Powhatan Arrow. *Mixed into the lightweight "consist" is a heavyweight diner, right in front of the round-end observation car.*

designers" who streamlined not only things that moved, such as trains, planes, cars, and ships, but also appliances and household items, such as refrigerators and vacuum cleaners.

A Pair of "Vest-Pocket" Streamliners

Railroading entered the streamline era in 1934 with two little trains — "lightweights" as opposed to heavyweights — that broke dramatically with the past. One was Union Pacific's M-10000, also simply called *Streamliner* and — later, when it entered regular service — the *City of Salina*. Made largely of aluminum, this train was built by the same Pullman Company that had dominated in the heavyweight era. It was colorful, painted a bright yellow with brown and red accents.

Completed just months after the M-10000 was Chicago, Burlington & Quincy's *Zephyr*. Like the UP train, it was articulated, meaning that the cars were permanently coupled together and shared wheel-sets under those couplings. Both trains were tiny — low-slung for speed, each just three cars long, including the power car. Both were intended for short, daylight runs. Both were major departures from existing passenger-train technology, and both generated great interest among travelers.

Though these similarities were striking, the differences were even more so. The *Zephyr* was built by the Edward G. Budd Manufacturing Company, new to railroad-car building. Budd used a different lightweight alloy — stainless steel — for his train, and developed a patented process called "shotwelding" to assemble it. The *Zephyr* would be unpainted, its fluted stainless steel making it a dramatic silver streak.

Another important difference was the powering of the two trains. The *Zephyr* had a diesel engine, a type of internal-combustion power plant just being perfected in a form light enough for railroad use. In order to be the very first streamliner, the M-10000 settled for an inferior engine that burned distillate (a petroleum product similar to gasoline).

Diesel proved far superior and came to power all streamliners other than the relatively few that employed steam or electric locomotives. ("Diesel" locomotives are more accurately called "diesel-electrics," since the diesel engines generate electricity, which is what actually drives the locomotives.)

More Streamliners, and Bigger Ones

The *Zephyr* and *Streamliner* were hugely successful, but they were simply too small. They couldn't carry enough passengers, and they didn't have enough space aboard to provide the luxuries rail passengers had come to expect, such features as dining cars, lounge cars, and sleeping cars.

Delaware & Hudson's New York City–Montreal Laurentian *(named for a mountain range near Montreal) rolls past a frozen Lake Champlain.*

Naming Trains

Passenger trains always have numbers, which are used by the railroaders who operate them. Since the early years, however, important trains have had names as well. In fact, the term "name train" means one with prestige — as does "limited" (because it is an "express" rather than a local train, making a limited number of stops). The term "limited" is part of some of the greatest train names: the *Broadway Limited*, the *20th Century Limited*, the Illinois Central's *Panama Limited*, the Northern Pacific's *North Coast Limited*, and many more.

The story of the *Zephyr's* naming is among the most unusual. Burlington executives were searching for a name for their new streamliner when one of them, believing that the train would be the "last word" in passenger railroading, suggested looking in the dictionary among the Zs. That led them to Zephyrus, the god of the west wind in Greek mythology — hence *Zephyr*.

Trains have gotten their names from many sources. A few were named for people. There was a *Mark Twain Zephyr*, a *Sam Houston Zephyr*, and a *General Pershing Zephyr*. The Alton Route ran the *Abraham Lincoln*. Great Northern's *Empire Builder* was named for James J. Hill, a famous GN executive widely know as the "Empire Builder."

Australia's Indian Pacific — *a transcontinental service linking those two ▶ oceans — was rare in carrying its name on its cars' sides.*

Especially in the streamline era, a number of railroads developed fleets of like-named trains. In addition to the *Zephyrs* and Union Pacific's *City* trains, there were Rock Island's *Rockets*, Southern Pacific's *Daylights*, and Santa Fe's *Chiefs*.

The "consist" (or make-up) of most great trains included at the rear an observation car — with open platforms in the wooden and heavyweight eras and enclosed, rounded ends in streamlined times. Attached would be an ornate "tailsign" (if rectangular) or "drumhead" (if round) bearing the train's name — the ultimate touch of class.

Southern Railway's Crescent Limited *ran to New Orleans, nicknamed the "Crescent City" because of its location on a broad bend of the Mississippi River.*

24 ∎ *Three railroads shared in the operation of the Chicago–San Francisco California Zephyr. Here the train runs through Colorado on the Denver & Rio Grande Western.*

So streamliners grew in size to meet these expectations, and to meet demand, since the public clearly preferred these sleek, colorful new trains to the old conventional ones. Burlington ordered more and bigger *Zephyrs* from Budd. Union Pacific introduced a whole fleet of trains named for destination cities: the *City of Portland*, *City of Los Angeles*, *City of San Francisco*, *City of Denver*. Soon virtually every major railroad was scrambling to join the streamline era.

After World War II, all the nation's railroads once more reequipped their passenger trains, which were threadbare after meeting wartime's unprecedented demands to move both troops and civilians. Many existing trains received spiffy new cars, and some all-new trains were launched as well. Among them was the *California Zephyr*, perhaps the most famous of all trains carrying dome cars, the last great innovation in long-distance, luxury rail travel.

These new trains gave passenger railroading one last boost, keeping the industry relatively healthy through the 1950s; but the handwriting was on the wall. Jets began to supplant propeller-driven aircraft. In 1956 President Dwight Eisenhower signed the Interstate Highway Act, assuring that automobiles would be the prime beneficiary of public money spent on transportation. Americans loved the independence their cars offered, and the speed of airplanes.

In the 1960s, most of America's great trains were discontinued as riders turned away and railroads lost interest. Santa Fe's famous *Chief* vanished, as did the *20th Century Limited* and Lackawanna's *Phoebe Snow*. Finally, in 1970, even the *California Zephyr* was allowed to die — a loss so shocking that politicians, journalists, and the public finally sat up and took notice. The result was Amtrak, the quasi-governmental corporation that in 1971 took over virtually all the nation's passenger trains.

Though introduced in 1955, six years after the California Zephyr, *Canadian Pacific's transcontinental* Canadian *— here making a winter journey through the mountains of British Columbia — used cars virtually identical to the CZ's.*

The Dome Car

On the Fourth of July in 1944, Cyrus Osborn — a General Motors vice president and general manger of that company's Electro-Motive Division, which built diesel locomotives — was riding one of those locomotives across Colorado. In beautiful Glenwood Canyon, carved by the Colorado River, he was struck by his unobstructed view through the broad windshield. "If people knew what they could see from here," Osborn said to the engineer, "they would pay $500, just to sit in the fireman's seat from Chicago to the West Coast."

Osborn was onto something, and that very night he made the first rough sketch of what would be a dome car — the best sightseeing vehicle ever made. Osborn took the idea to his colleagues, who were impressed enough that General Motors agreed to help design and sponsor the *Train of Tomorrow*. Built by Pullman-Standard (part of the old Pullman Company) and completed in 1947, this demonstrator train had four cars, all with domes. It barnstormed around the country for four years, attracting huge crowds, before being bought by Union Pacific.

Built by the Budd Company for Canadian Pacific's Canadian, *this dome-observation is seen here running in Nova Scotia for VIA, the company currently operating Canada's passenger trains. Canadian Pacific named cars of this type for national or provincial parks.*

However, in 1945, the Burlington Route had taken one of its Budd-built day coaches and added a dome in its own shops. The resulting *Silver Dome* was the first by far and led to an extensive fleet of dome-carrying *Zephyrs*.

All told, 236 dome cars were built, for only sixteen railroads (though others would acquire some second-hand). Almost all were in the West, since tunnels and bridges on most Eastern lines were too low to accommodate them. By whatever name — Burlington called them "Vista-Domes," Union Pacific "Astra Domes," Canadian Pacific "Scenic Domes," others "Planetarium Domes," "Strata Domes," "Pleasure Domes," "Great Domes," or "Big Domes" — these cars were a delight.

The view from domes like this "Park car" on the Canadian *is often spectacular.*

Today some dome cars are operated by excursion railroads such as Pennsylvania's Reading & Northern.

Three

Amtrak, Our Nation's Railroad

ON MAY 1, 1971, AMTRAK WAS BORN into what has proven to be a hard-knock existence. Created by Congress to take over the tattered remnants of America's once-grand passenger rail system, it was an institution with an unclear mission and not enough money. Some critics felt that it was designed to fail — that it was intended as a graceful way for the passenger train to die a blameless death, reflecting no discredit on government leaders.

By 1970, virtually no American railroad wanted to run passenger trains, which had turned into chronic money-losers. Amtrak was their way out. By paying a fee, railroads would be freed of their obligation to run passenger trains and could concentrate on hauling freight, which was where the profits were. They might be able to sell their equipment to Amtrak — the corporation would need some twelve hundred cars and three hundred locomotives — and, if their routes were selected as part of the Amtrak system, make a small profit operating Amtrak's trains. (At first, Amtrak owned none of the tracks it used. Now it owns the "Northeast Corridor" lines — Washington, D.C., to New York and Boston, along with the spur from Philadelphia to Harrisburg, Pennsylvania.)

◀ *Amtrak's version of the* California Zephyr *runs along the Fraser River in Colorado.*

Twenty railroads chose to join Amtrak, while three — Southern, Rock Island, and Rio Grande — originally stayed out. (All have since joined.) Right from the beginning, Amtrak had problems. Its first president, Roger Lewis, had no previous railroad experience. Much of the equipment it inherited was shoddy and run-down. Air conditioning frequently failed.

New Equipment Helps Amtrak

Amtrak's first new coaches, for the Northeast Corridor and other short-haul service, were tubular aircraftlike cars called "Amfleet," introduced in 1975. These utilitarian cars have small windows that diminish sightseeing pleasure.

Amtrak's next new cars, bilevels dubbed "Superliners," were far more successful. Delivered beginning in 1979, they include chair cars (coaches), sleepers, diners, and "Sightseer" lounges. With broad windows and some overhead glass, these lounges are a replacement for domes, which aren't a possibility on cars that already are double-deckers. Similar but single-level sleepers called "Viewliners" now run on trains serving New York City, where tunnels are too tight for Superliners. Amtrak's newest equipment is the sleek Acela trainsets designed for high-speed service between Washington and Boston.

The *California Zephyr* still provides America's most scenic journey, from Chicago to Denver, through the Rocky Mountains and along the Colorado River to Salt Lake City, and over the Sierras to Oakland (across the bay from San Francisco). The *Empire Builder* keeps another famous name alive in the Northwest, running between Chicago and Seattle and Portland. The *Southwest Chief*, the *Texas Eagle*, and the *Sunset Limited* provide service between Los Angeles and the Midwest and Southeast. These trains all feature Superliner cars, as does the Chicago–New Orleans *City of New Orleans* and the Los Angeles–Seattle *Coast Starlight*.

Not all the great Amtrak scenery is in the West. The New York–Montreal *Adirondack* makes an all-day trip along the Hudson River and Lake Champlain, while the New York–Chicago *Cardinal* runs through West Virginia's New River Gorge.

Throughout its existence, Amtrak has struggled for funding, always fighting the unreasonable expectation that it turn a profit. (All passenger trains throughout the world rely on some form of government support, as do all transportation modes in the United States.) In spite of its financial problems, however, the corporation has continued to run trains that retain most of the pleasures of rail travel — dining cars and sleeping cars in particular, but also just the inherent delight of whisking through the countryside on that magic carpet made of steel.

This "Sightseer" lounge is part of the Washington-Chicago Capitol Limited.

Acela Means "Acceleration" and "Excellence"

The United States didn't enter the world of high-speed passenger railroading until nearly four decades after the Japanese had begun it in 1964 with the Shinkansen. Popularly called the "Bullet Train," it ran at first between Tokyo and Osaka at speeds up to 131 miles per hour over tracks designed especially for it. It now serves other routes as well.

Beginning in 1981, the French stepped to the fore with their TGV or Train à Grande Vitesse, which means "train of great speed." Sleek TGV trainsets built by a French-based company called Alstom now criss-cross France on a network of routes.

For the Acela Express, its first true high-speed train, Amtrak turned to Alstom for the design and hired Bombardier, a Canadian company, to construct the trainsets in Barre, Vermont. Ever since these long-awaited, much-publicized trains entered service between Washington and Boston in 2000, they have been dogged by mechanical problems. Still, they provide a highly pleasurable ride and are especially popular with business travelers.

The Acela trainsets are eight cars long, with a power unit at each end. Like some other high-speed trains (but not Alstom's TGVs), they have a tilting mechanism to get them comfortably through the numerous curves on the route. (Building a straighter right-of-way just for high-speed trains — as the Japanese and French did — was impractical in the densely populated northeastern United States.)

Acela Express trains are powered by electricity, drawn from overhead wires called "catenary." Though these wires were in place from Washington to New York and on to New Haven, electrification from New Haven northeast to Boston was part of the Acela project.

Though Acela Express trains briefly hit a top speed of 150 miles an hour, they make most of their two-hour-and-forty-minute Washington–New York and three-hour-and-thirty-minute Boston–New York journeys at a substantially slower pace. Still, the coaches are spacious and comfortable, with broad windows and up-to-date styling. Now, at last, passengers whisked along the Northeast Corridor can feel that modern railroading has come to America.

An Acela Express rolls into Boston's South Station.

Four

Oh Canada!
Riding Northern Rails

CANADA IS A VAST COUNTRY, with lots of surviving wilderness but a population far smaller than that of the United States. It's also a country that thinks railroads are an essential part of its heritage. British Columbia, the westernmost province, joined the Canadian Confederation only when promised that it would be linked to the rest of the country by a railroad. This first transcontinental line, the Canadian Pacific, was completed in 1885.

Competing railroads eventually were built, but before long they failed and were grouped together as the government-run Canadian National (which only recently became a private corporation). Throughout the middle years of the twentieth century, CP and CN ran most of Canada's passenger trains.

Canadian trains have always been much like those in the United States, so it's no wonder that Canadian and American passenger trains met similar fates. As ridership diminished on CP and CN, VIA Rail Canada (a company similar to Amtrak) was formed in 1976 to

◀ Banff Park, *the dome-observation aboard VIA's* Atlantic, *glows a cozy welcome.*   ■ *33*

In 1973, before VIA's formation, a Canadian National train headed for Montreal crosses the Richelieu River in the Province of Quebec.

shoulder the burden of running Canada's passenger trains. Like Amtrak, VIA has had its ups and downs. The worst of the downs came in January 1990, when the country lost half its passenger-train service. In spite of that, VIA still operates some wonderful trains. Even today passengers can travel all the way from Vancouver on the West Coast to Halifax on the East Coast by rail.

The Canadian: An Elegant, Old-Fashioned Streamliner

VIA's flagship and one of the world's greatest passenger trains, the *Canadian*, runs three days each week between Vancouver and Toronto. Inaugurated by Canadian Pacific half a century ago, this train still uses its original 1955 equipment.

It remains a classic stainless-steel streamliner, a direct descendant of the 1934 *Zephyr*, with shiny fluted sides.

When the Canadian's cars were renovated in the early 1990s, heating and electrical systems were changed completely. Dating back to the time of steam locomotives, trains had been heated by steam. When diesels replaced steamers, those that hauled passenger trains were equipped with "steam-generators," just to provide heating for the coaches. By the 1980s, however, this mode had become obsolete and was replaced by a system of "head-end power," with the diesel locomotive generating electric power for heat, lights, and air conditioning (as well as to drive the traction motors that pulled the train). Thus the refurbished *Canadian* was HEP-equipped, better in the teeth of frigid northern winters.

The *Canadian* has all the elements that make train travel great fun: sleeping cars, dining cars, dome cars, and an observation car. In addition, it makes a long, leisurely journey across the sweeping beauty of Canada. In the course of three days, the train conquers the western mountains, races across the prairies, and winds through the rugged "Canadian Shield," a wilderness of lakes, rivers, swamps, and rock outcrops left by receding glaciers.

VIA runs other fine trains, too, including frequent service in Canada's most densely settled heart — between Quebec City, Montreal, Ottawa, Toronto, and Windsor, Ontario. These trains use more modern LRC (which stands for "Light, Rapid, Comfortable") cars, or brand-new Renaissance equipment, built by Alstom for service through Europe's Channel Tunnel but never used there.

The eastbound Canadian, *at left, is ready to leave Vancouver. The recently arrived* ▶ *westbound is on the adjacent track. The wreath of steam shows that the trains have not yet been converted to head-end power.*

Steward Hans Knepper welcomes guests to the Canadian's *dining car.*

Five

Europe— Still a Railroad Continent

NORTH AMERICA IS HUGE, which has made it difficult in the modern era for American and Canadian passenger trains to compete with jet airplanes. Europe, on the other hand, is compact. Its dozens of countries as a group could fit comfortably within the footprint of just a few of our largest states or provinces. This has made it a perfect place for passenger railroading.

So while North America's passenger trains struggled in the last decades of the twentieth century, Europe's flourished. With France, Germany, Belgium, Spain, and Italy leading the way, high-speed trains popped up across the Continent. In 1994 the rail-only Channel Tunnel opened between England and France, and fast Eurostar trains began running from London to Paris and Brussels. Country after country made a commitment to rail as the perfect way to fight congestion on the highways and in the skies.

Today, most major European airports connect directly with the rail network. In cities and villages alike, fine hotels are located right by the railway station, as they have been since the railway age began. Both residents and tourists can manage without an automobile — something nearly impossible in the United States.

◀ *In Switzerland, the narrow-gauge* Glacier Express *links the resort cities of Zermatt and St. Moritz with Chur and Brig. "FO" stands for Furka Oberalp, one of the three independent railroads that team up to operate the train.*

Germany's sleek, high-speed ICEs sometimes run internationally. This one is in Switzerland, entering Zurich's Hauptbahnhof.

The upper-level deluxe compartments of CityNightLine trains are almost like dome cars, with overhead glass.

Europe's Rail Renaissance Begins

There was a time when North America's passenger trains generally outshone Europe's in comfort, speed, and luxury. In 1957 that began to change with the introduction of the Trans-European Expresses. These flashy trains were all first-class. They were fast (by the standards of the day), making only limited stops. Not constrained by borders, they were international. Until their gradual replacement after three decades by EuroCity trains (similarly international, but carrying both first- and second-class cars), they represented the best of European train travel.

EuroCity trains — clean, comfortable, fast, frequent, dependable — are the workhorses. The thoroughbreds are the various high-speed services, led by France's TGVs. Germany has its ICEs (Inter-City Expresses), Belgium its Thalys, Sweden its X2000s, Spain its Talgo 200s and AVEs, Italy and Switzerland their Cisalpino.

Fast is important, but so is frequent and far-flung. Visit a hub like Zurich's Hauptbahnhof (main railway station) and you'll see a dizzying array of trains — locomotives and coaches of many different shapes and colors — headed for the four corners of Europe. Overnight Talgo "Trenhotels" (hotel trains) leave for Spain. ICEs sprint to major German cities. Fancy CityNightLine sleepers also serve Germany — Hamburg, Berlin, and Dresden. Trains head over Arlberg Pass into Austria. They go to Milan, Paris, Geneva, Brussels, Amsterdam, Prague. They go to every corner of Switzerland. Standing on the station platform in Zurich is like watching a three-ring circus of trains.

The meter-gauge Rhaetian Railway's Bernina Express *runs from Chur, in Switzerland, to Tirano, in Italy. Here it rolls past glaciers at Lago Bianca, "White Lake" in Italian.*

Switzerland's Little Trains

Speed is not the best thing about every European train. Some specialize in charm and scenery. This is especially true in Switzerland, where many lines wind through the Alps. The *Glacier Express*, for instance, connects Zermatt and St. Moritz, two famous ski resorts. The little train travels on "meter-gauge" tracks — with rails a little more than a yard apart, considerably smaller than "standard gauge," which is 4 feet 8½ inches. It was cheaper and easier to build through the mountains in this narrower gauge.

"A theme park for railfans" is what one guidebook author has called Switzerland. Unlike most European countries, which are dominated by single nationalized rail systems, Switzerland has roughly seventy independent lines supplementing the

Trains on Switzerland's Rigi Bahn use a "cog wheel" or gear that meshes with a ladderlike "rack rail" in the middle of the track to haul themselves up steep grades. Some of the trains are pushed by a steam locomotive.

In Europe, a single train often serves multiple destinations, splitting en route. Signs are hung on car sides (see also pages 36–37) to ensure that passengers board the proper car. Here these signs are racked up at Zurich Hauptbahnhof.

A sleek French TGV rolls into the railway station in Marseille. When the first TGV line opened in 1981, it marked the beginning of high-speed rail service in Europe. Since then, many other countries have added high-speed trains.

Swiss Federal Railways. Each has its own equipment and color scheme. The *Glacier Express*, for instance, is operated by three independent lines: the Brig-Visp-Zermatt, the Furka-Oberalp, and the Rhaetian Railway.

The Rhaetian Railway is perhaps the most dramatic of all. Some of Switzerland's mountain railways use "rack and pinion" to climb up steep grades. This mode has a "cog wheel," or gear, turning with the axles and meshing with a toothed center rail, pulling the train along as if it were climbing a ladder. In contrast, the Rhaetian uses regular "adhesion" traction, with locomotive wheels turning to provide the power. To achieve the lesser grades required by this mode, the railway uses spectacular stone bridges, tunnels, and loops.

Another of Switzerland's steep and scenic meter-gauge

railways is the Montreux-Oberland-Bernois. On it runs the high-tech *Crystal Panoramic Express*, which has a passenger compartment in front that offers an engineer's-eye view.

Switzerland has an abundance of hydroelectric power. Most of its rail lines host frequent passenger service. These characteristics make it a natural for electrification, so virtually all its railways are strung with catenary and run on electricity. On a few mountain railways, however, steam locomotives survive, primarily because they are attractive to the tourists who ride these lines.

Whether meter-gauge or standard, Swiss or Swedish or any nationality in between, today's trains make Europe a rail wonderland.

Magnificent Stations and Humble Depots

In America, the village depot was once a centerpiece of small-town life, both a gathering place and a link to the outside world. Imposing city stations were monuments to travel and were beehives of activity.

Though magnificently refurbished Washington Union Station and Grand Central Terminal in New York City are nearly as bustling as ever, many train stations in the United States have closed. In Europe, in contrast, most railway stations are as busy as ever, awash in commuters and long-distance travelers alike.

Both the railroads that built them and the communities they serve have regarded stations as a measure of their own importance. Corporate and communal pride typically lie behind these portals to rail travel. Railroads employed the finest architects. "Make no little plans," said Daniel H. Burnham, who designed Washington Union Station and many of Chicago's most famous skyscrapers as well. Work on Grand Central required two famous architectural firms. In Finland, Helsinki's station is the work of world-famous Eliel Saarinen.

Railroad stations, large and small, have always had an electricity, full as they are of the sorrow of parting and the joy and adventure of travel.

Saarinen's magnificent station in Helsinki.

NJ Transit trains, typical of the commuter runs that still funnel into many major cities in the United States, serve this modest depot in Hillsdale, New Jersey.

Six

Riding the Rails for Fun

CUNARD LINE, AMONG THE WORLD'S foremost steamship companies, has claimed that "getting there is half the fun" — a sentiment true of rail as well as sea travel. In fact, for some of today's trains, the on-board experience — rather than transportation from one place to another — is the main purpose of traveling. Such trains are like cruise ships, which blossomed in popularity after ships making point-to-point "line voyages" virtually disappeared.

No sooner had we stopped routinely using ships and trains for practical travel, it seems, than we missed them — and began riding just for fun.

Actually, excursion trains have been around for a long time. A century ago, Colorado railroads ran "wildflower excursions," taking passengers on daylong trips to pick mountain wildflowers. In 1869 a cog railway was built in New Hampshire to take excursionists to the top of Mount Washington and back. That railroad is going strong today.

Aboard the luxury Venice Simplon-Orient-Express, *passengers await their meals in a dining car ornamented with glass panels by noted designer René Lalique. Fine linen, china, crystal, and silverware characterize the service.*

Sailing on the Cruise Trains

However, recreational railroading is more common today than ever before. Dinner in the diner is such a pleasant experience that "dinner trains," where a short train ride serves primarily as a setting for a meal, have sprung up. Luxury trains are another aspect of this rail rebirth. In Britain there's the *Royal Scotsman*, in Thailand and Malaysia the *Eastern & Oriental Express*, in India the *Palace on Wheels*, and in South Africa Rovos Rail's *Pride of Africa*, *Blue Train*, and *Union Limited*. Here in North America, the *American Orient Express* offers nine different itineraries, most a week long, which cover some Amtrak routes and various freight-only railroads.

The *AOE*, as it's known for short, is just like a cruise ship on rails, stopping at numerous "ports" along the way so passengers can disembark and take tours. The train, with interiors decorated to suggest European elegance of years gone by, were built in the middle of the twentieth century for the great American streamliners.

The Venice Simplon-Orient-Express *pauses at St. Anton am Arlberg, high in the Austrian Alps.*

"Double-headed" steam locomotives lead the Union Limited *tour train in South Africa.*

The *AOE* borrows the name of perhaps the most famous train ever, the *Orient Express.* Beginning in 1883, it ran from Paris to Istanbul, then called Constantinople. (This city lies on the Bosporus, the strait that divides Europe from Asia, or the Orient, hence the train's name.) The *Orient Express* was operated by La Compagnie Internationale des Wagons-Lits et des Grands Express Européens. This name, which translates roughly as the international company of sleeping cars and great European express trains, is so long that the company was typically known just as "Wagons-Lits." It was founded by Georges Nagelmachers, a Belgian, who was Europe's George Pullman.

The original *Orient Express* was discontinued in 1977 but reborn in 1983 as the *Venice Simplon-Orient-Express,* a fancy excursion operated with the original cars, refurbished at great expense. They are the height of elegance, with inlaid wood. In fact, the *VSOE* is a rolling museum. Meals and service are very posh. Passengers dress up for dinner, sometimes in period costumes.

Excursions Keep Steam Locomotives Alive

Of course, many rail excursions are much less opulent than this — and far less costly to ride. Throughout the United States, and in many other countries as well, railroads offer tourists and railfans the chance to climb aboard and take a ride just for fun. Often such trips feature great scenery. In Colorado, for instance, you can take a train deep into the heart of the steep, craggy Royal Gorge, carved by the Arkansas River; over a high, curved metal trestle on the Georgetown Loop Railroad; through Animas Canyon on the Durango & Silverton Narrow-Gauge Railroad; or up steep grades and around curve after curve on the Cumbres & Toltec Scenic Railroad.

The last three of these have an added attraction — a steam locomotive up front. The smell of coal smoke, the mournful whistle, the purposeful chugging as the train surges along: All this is part of the delight of steam railroading. Happily, it's available on many excursion trains around the world. There's the Harzer Schmalspur Bahnen. ("Schmalspur Bahnen" means narrow-gauge railway; this one runs in the Harz Mountains of Germany.) There's Puffing Billy in Australia, and the Zig-Zag Railway. Great Britain hosts many preserved lines with steam, including a handful of tiny narrow-gauge routes in Wales.

Tourist trains are scattered across the United States. You can ride one — behind a steam locomotive or historic diesel — to the South Rim of the Grand Canyon. Pennsylvania has a number of steam-operated lines, including Steamtown (run by the National Park Service); the Strasburg Rail Road (the oldest short-line railroad in the country); the East Broad Top, New Hope & Ivyland; and Wanamaker, Kempton & Southern. The most northerly excursion route is the White Pass & Yukon, which runs inland from the port of Skagway, Alaska.

In addition, main-line railroads sometimes host excursions, though not as frequently as they once did. All things considered, though, many opportunities to ride the rails do remain. In many instances, trains are still a fine way to get from one place to another. In other instances, they're just fun to be aboard. In all cases, there's inescapably a magic about feeling the rumble of wheels underfoot, about being gently jostled in your seat by the rhythm of the rails, about watching the world stream by through the perfect picture frame of a coach window.

Five dome cars offer great views to passengers aboard a "Montana by Steam" excursion.

Glossary

Amfleet: Amtrak's first new passenger equipment, single-level cars delivered by The Budd Company beginning in 1975.

Conductor: The "captain" of the train and ultimate authority who rides aboard and collects tickets. Called the "guard" in Great Britain and Europe.

Consist (pronounced CON-sist): The arrangement of cars in a train.

Dome car: A car with a bubblelike glass extension on top in which passengers sit for unsurpassed viewing.

Double bedroom: A sleeping room for two, with daytime seating that converts to upper and lower berths at night.

Drumhead: A round sign bearing the train's name that hangs on the rear of an observation car.

Express train: A fast passenger train making few stops.

Gauge (standard, meter): Distance between the inside of the rails. Standard is 4 feet 8$1/2$ inches.

Head-end power (HEP): Electricity for a train's lighting, heating, and air conditioning generated by diesel engines aboard the locomotive.

Heavyweight car: A railroad passenger car built of riveted steel, typically riding on six-wheel trucks.

Industrial designers: Professionals who, beginning especially in the 1930s, made a wide variety of products and vehicles more functional and attractive, often through streamlining.

Lightweight car: A railroad passenger car made of light metals or alloys, typically stainless steel or (less commonly) aluminum, that was streamlined in shape and modern in appearance.

Limited: A fast train making a limited number of stops.

Make up/make down (berths): To convert sleeping-car spaces to beds for overnight or seats for day use.

Observation car: A car at the end of the train that, in the heavyweight era, featured a railed open platform and, in the streamliner era, a bullet- or blunt-end lounge with rear-facing windows.

Open section: A Pullman accommodation featuring facing seats that were made down at night into upper and lower berths, then hung with heavy curtains for privacy.

Porter: A sleeping-car attendant.

Pullman car: In North America, a sleeping car. In Great Britain and Europe, a luxurious day accommodation.

Rack and pinion: A cog wheel that meshes with a ladderlike center rail to allow trains to climb steep grades.

Sightseer lounge: An Amtrak double-deck Superliner car with overhead windows suggestive of a dome car.

Streamliner: A sleek, aerodynamically efficient style of train, light in weight, that was introduced in the 1930s.

Superliner: Amtrak bilevel cars, introduced in 1979, used on most western trains.

Tailsign: A sign, like a drumhead but square, bearing the train's name that hangs on the rear of an observation car.

Viewliner: Amtrak's single-level sleeping car, dating from 1996, used on long-distance trains that run through the tunnels into New York City.

Index